Iola Ferris

My Life Far Away

Adventures in Cambodia

ជីវិតរបស់ខ្ញុំនៅឆ្ងាយ

ដំណើរផ្សងព្រេងក្នុងប្រទេសកម្ពុជា

A true story

Tola Ferris

INFINITY
PUBLISHING.COM

ISBN 978-0-7414-5235-1

Published by:

PUBLISHING.COM

1094 New DeHaven Street, Suite 100
West Conshohocken, PA 19428-2713
Info@buybooksontheweb.com
www.buybooksontheweb.com
Toll-free (877) BUY BOOK
Local Phone (610) 941-9999
Fax (610) 941-9959

Printed in the United States of America

Published December 2013

To my loving father

I would not be here right now if it weren't for you.
Dad, thanks for adopting me and sharing your amazing
family with me. I love you more than words can say.

Foreword

by my father

I was honored when Tola asked me to write a foreword for her book. It is a privilege to share some of what I was going through half a world away during her early life in Cambodia.

I had always wanted to have a family. Eventually I realized that if I was going to have one, the only legal and moral way would be to adopt. As I checked into it, some encouraged me; others didn't. So, I prayed. More than once.

One day I attended a meeting on adoption. The people there agreed that it was indeed legal, but they didn't like the idea. So, on the way home, I prayed again. A few minutes later, I got the strangest feeling that I *knew* it would happen. I can't explain it, but somehow I *knew*. I just didn't know how or when. Meanwhile, life went on.

After reading, considering, and asking lots of questions, I contacted some agencies. Finally, a woman at an agency suggested adopting from Cambodia. There were other options, but since I already knew a little about Cambodia, I thought, "Why not?" Next thing I knew, I was busy with all the requirements and paperwork needed by both the U.S. and Cambodia. A few months later it was done.

One evening after work, I got a phone call from my contact at the agency. She asked if I would be interested in adopting a six-year-old named Tola. I agreed, and started the preparations for a trip to Cambodia.

A couple months later, about 3:00 on a Thursday morning, I got a phone call from my contact in Cambodia. She said that everything was ready, and to come and get Tola. After a very busy three days of packing and making final arrangements for travel, I was on my way. Thirty hours later, I got off the plane in Phnom Penh, Cambodia, and met my contact, a fair-skinned American lady with a tropical tan. From there, her driver, Pol, took us out to an orphanage about 45 minutes away.

Near the end of our ride, we turned right and continued down a quiet shady street. We passed a long white wall on our left. Soon we came to a gate in the wall, and we drove inside. We parked in front of a big white building and got out. As we did, a petite, pretty Cambodian lady came around the corner. A small girl was walking with her. My contact informed me that this was Tola, my new daughter, and introduced me to her as her dad. At that point, Tola hurried around to the other side of the Cambodian lady and peeked out at me shyly from behind her leg.

Seven years after I *knew* that I would have a family, almost to the day, I had met my daughter. A prayer answered. A new beginning.

Index of Names*
តារាងរាយឈ្មោះ

These people were a significant part of my life in Cambodia.

Srey and **Nimol** (SRY and ni-MOL) I thought of them as my parents.
Kaipiset (KY-pee-set) He was Srey and Nimol's son. I considered him my brother.

A'aom (ah-OWM) I called him my brother, but he wasn't related to me.

Bongno and **Bongnan** (bong-NO and bong-NAHN) They were sisters, about ten years older than me. I called them my cousins, but they weren't related to me. They cared about me a lot.

Kahan and **Knuu** (ka-HAHN and k'NOO) They were sisters, close to my age.
Kchrap (k'CHRAHP) She played with Kahan, Knuu, and me a lot.

Ne' Kruu **Sawk** (ne' kroo SAWK) He was my schoolteacher.

Seinique (say-NEEK) She was half French and half Cambodian. She was my best friend.
Ma' Lee (ma' LEE) She worked for the orphanage. She was Seinique's mother.

Min 'Iep (meen 'EE-ep) She worked at the orphanage.

*Some names have been changed.

Prologue

បុរេកថា

I was born in Phnom Penh, Cambodia. I was told that my biological parents had died, but I never found out how. This happened so early in my life that I don't have any memory of them. My earliest memory was of a time when I was living with a lady in a small village. It had been a long time before, and I don't remember much about her. I knew that she wasn't my mother, and I didn't live with her very long.

One day she brought me to live with a new family about an hour's walk away. They lived in a house made of bamboo near the edge of the jungle. I spent most of my time with them, and I soon thought of them as my parents.

I had no idea what adventures awaited me.

First Memories

អនុស្សាវរីយ៍ដំបូង

The wind picked up, and the clouds started rolling in. I sat on the wooden fence that surrounded the property, letting the breeze go through my hair. It was about to rain, but I wanted to spend a few more moments outside because it felt so good. Then my mom called to me from inside the house. I ran inside, and a second later the rain began pouring down. I watched the rain through the doorway. The raindrops were huge and came down hard. I could feel the prickles of rain coming down through the thatched palm roof. It was slightly cool, but it felt good. My parents, Nimol and Srey, were getting ready to go to sleep.

My house was made of bamboo and palm leaves. It didn't have a door. There was a wooden shelf built about two feet off the ground that they used as a bed. I had to sleep on the ground because there was no room for me on the bed. It wasn't that comfortable, but I always fell asleep fast and woke up rested. Whenever it rained, I would wake up with dirt stuck to my cheek.

A little ways in front of my house there were some lime bushes. I liked to pick them and bite into them. Then I would throw them away because they were sour. Even though I didn't like them, I still kept biting into them and tossing them away. It was like a game.

Our neighbors lived in a house on stilts a few feet away from ours. On the other side of their house there were some sugar cane plants. Sometimes my neighbor would cut down a stalk of sugar cane, and he would give me a piece. It was sweeter than anything I had ever eaten. It was crispy, and it had a nice crunch when I bit into it.

Beyond their house, about a hundred feet away, they had a field of rice and onions. I liked to walk around there right after it rained and feel the mud squish between my toes.

A few feet in front of their house, they had a well where we got water for cooking our food. It was more convenient to have water close by than walking into the jungle to the river and back again.

There was a patch of cucumbers that grew up between our houses. I liked to pick them and eat them. Usually I would share one with my friend.

Sometimes my parents would ask me to go mushroom hunting. They would give me a basket, and I would ask my friend next door if she wanted to come along. She always did. She was about my age, and she had curly brown hair. We would walk deep into the jungle to a clearing where they grew, and we would pick them. We would try to see how many we could fit into the basket without them falling out.

During the monsoon season it would rain almost everyday nonstop. Sometimes during this time, my neighbor's daughter and I would run around naked in the rain. We had a lot of fun sloshing through the mud and watching the worms. Other times I would go outside naked with a bar of soap and take a bath in the rain.

One night I was leaning against a stack of hay bales, looking up at the stars. I was wondering how I came to be. I came to the conclusion that I had somehow fallen from the sky, and there I was. While I was thinking about this, a memory came to me of the time I was living with another lady. She was the one who had brought me to live with Nimol and Srey.

One time she came back to my new house and took me to a small building on stilts. Inside there were five *proh ong* (Buddhist priests). They were sitting in a row in front of some other regular people. They were dressed in orange robes, and their heads were shaved.

The lady I came with had brought some food in a stack of three metal containers. They were about five inches wide, and together they were about a foot and a half tall. They were a special set of containers only used for the *proh ong*. She placed them in front of one of the *proh ong*. The others already had metal containers in front of them. They bowed their heads, closed their eyes, and started to pray. Everybody else put their hands together in a praying fashion and bowed their heads. I didn't understand what was going on. The *proh ong* started mumbling words, but I couldn't understand any of it. I soon lost interest and looked out the door. There was nothing interesting going on outside either, so I decided to try praying like everyone else. I had a hard time trying to cross my legs, so I gave up. It seemed like hours until the *proh ong* were done praying.

When they finished, they opened the containers of food. They all did this at exactly the same moment. The aroma of the food was amazing. It made my mouth water, and I longed for a taste of it. The *proh ong* then took a bite of each item of food and put it in their mouths at exactly the same moment. I was fascinated by this. After trying every item in that container, they would pass the containers down, and the process would begin again until every *proh ong* had tried every container. The containers were then handed back to their original owners. We went outside, and the lady shared the rest of the food with me. It tasted even better than it smelled. It was the best food I had ever had.

The lady that had taken me to see the *proh ong* came back another day and took me to her village. She took me inside her house. There were other girls around, and they were dancing. The lady showed me how to do a traditional Cambodian dance, and I practiced with the other girls. She brought me to her house several times for dance lessons. Then she stopped coming for me, and I never found out why. I enjoyed dancing, and I wanted to learn more.

It was that time of year again. The end of the monsoon season had come, and the water had started to subside. During this time when the rivers weren't flooding, the people would celebrate. It was a day called *Bon Om Tuk* (the Water Festival). Many people would gather at a certain place, and they would cook food all day in the largest pots I had ever seen. The pots were about a foot and a half wide and two feet high. There were about fifty people cooking because they were preparing a meal for several hundred people. Some people would gather mangos, pomegranates, and other tropical fruits. They would cut them into pieces for people to snack on until the main course of the meal was served.

While the grownups cooked, I would play games and climb trees with the other kids. Climbing trees was one of my favorite things to do. I could climb trees barefoot and not get hurt.

By the time the food was ready, it was almost dark. I was ravenous by then. People would gather up their bowls and walk to someone's big pot, and the person would serve them their soup. The food was always good. When everyone was sitting down, they would play music, and a few people would dance.

I went to the *Bon Om Tuk* grounds several times. There was a pomegranate tree there, and I liked to climb it and eat the fruit. The pomegranates were pretty, and they were always sweet and juicy.

Sometimes I would play on a stack of hay bales that was always there. It was about fifteen feet high. I loved to climb to the top because it was so high. When I reached the top, I would pick some of them up and stack them around me like walls. I would pretend that it was my house. Sometimes there would be another kid there, and we would try to make the house as big as we could.

Late one evening I had to wash clothes down by the river. I saw two young people across the river coming out of the jungle. They didn't seem to notice me at all, even though they were looking in my direction. They were holding hands and laughing loudly. They walked across the river with such grace that it surprised me. The current in the river was very strong. It would slow anyone down, but they kept walking forward as if there was no current at all. Not even my mother, who was stronger than me, could walk in the current with such grace as they did. The people walked toward me about half way across, took off to the left, and started wading upstream. I wondered why they were walking against the force of the water. I had never seen anyone do this before. When I looked closer at them, I noticed something strange. I could see right through them as if I was looking through clear water. I didn't know what to think of that.

While I watched, I heard a noise behind me. I turned around, and it was my cousin Bongno. She asked me what all the noise was. I pointed in the direction of where the people were, but when we looked, no one was there. This scared me a little. They had just vanished into thin air. I told Bongno what I had seen, and I described how gracefully they walked. Bongno told me to be careful because they were ghosts. She had told me stories before about ghosts walking around at night. She said that they were ghosts because people just can't disappear that fast. I didn't believe that they were ghosts, but it still gave me the creeps. Bongno picked up the basket and put the wet clothes in it. I told her that I wasn't done washing, but Bongno said she didn't want to be around when more ghosts came. I didn't see any harm in those people though. They had done nothing to me.

One afternoon my mom was about to have her baby. An old lady came to our house to help her receive it. I didn't quite understand what was going on. The old lady told me to go away, but I went around to the side of the house instead. I peeked through the bamboo wall and watched what was about to happen. The old lady held my mom's hand and told her something. My mom was lying on the wooden shelf that was used as a bed. She spread her legs apart and began to scream. I thought there was something wrong with her. I wanted to go inside and ask her what was wrong. I knew somehow that I shouldn't, so I just stayed where I was. My mom screamed some more. Then the old lady reached down and pulled something up to her. The thing cried, and I could see that it was covered in blood. I walked into the house, and my mom told me that it was a baby. The old woman wiped away the blood from its body, and she let my mom hold it. Its crying annoyed me, so I left.

A couple weeks after the baby was born, I found out that we were moving. I was sad because I would not see my friend any more. I had to carry a few small things. Srey carried the baby, and Nimol carried some larger items. After setting everything we had in front of our bamboo house, Nimol started to tear the house down. He said he didn't want anyone to live there when we left. I didn't understand why he wanted to do this. Nimol left the broken house there. I picked up what I had to carry, and we left. After passing the wooden gate, I paused and took one last look at the place where I used to live. I wanted to have one final memory of my old home. Then I followed my parents.

After a long walk, we came to a bridge. It was about two feet wide and fifty feet long. My parents walked across the bridge like it was no big deal. The bridge looked more like a long piece of wood. There were no railings on the sides, so I could have easily fallen off. As I walked slowly across, I could feel the bridge swaying. I tried not to look down, but I did anyway. My curiosity was stronger than my fears. It was a long drop down. The waves of the ocean made big splashes against the cliff. I could feel the spray from the surf on my face. It looked like the waves could engulf me alive. I felt dizzy, and I thought I was going to fall. Then I heard my parents yelling for me to hurry up. I ran the rest of the way across. The bridge moved even more when I ran, and that scared me. When I got safely across, I took a deep breath. My heart was still pounding. I was relieved to have reached the end of the bridge.

After I crossed the bridge, I looked around. To my left there was a dirt road for cars. I wished that I could have gone there. I could see the ocean on the right, but I thought it was a big river. Birds were flying everywhere. It was a beautiful sight.

We walked through the jungle for the rest of the day and into the night. We got to our new house after dark. It was much bigger than the bamboo house, and it was built on stilts. We had to use a ladder to climb up into it. It was different than my neighbor's house next to our old bamboo house. Their house wasn't as high, and their ladder was built into the house. This house had a ladder that could be removed. I set the items down that I had been carrying and started to climb up. The ladder started moving, and I almost fell to the side, but Nimol came and held the ladder for me. When we all got into the house, Nimol threw the ladder down. I wondered how we would get down in the morning. I was exhausted from the trip. I had never walked so far in my life. I lay my head down and fell asleep.

House On Stilts

ផ្ទះមានជើងសសរ

My new house was about ten feet square. There was no furniture in the house. The only things we had inside were our clothes and a blanket for the baby. The house had no windows, just an opening for the door. The roof was tilted up like a triangle and was made of palm leaves. There was a hole in the floor in one corner of the house. It was there so we could *chu-nóm* (pee) if we had to go in the middle of the night. I didn't go outside to *chu-nóm* because at night Nimol would take the ladder and push it to the ground. It was a dangerous jump to the ground for someone small like me.

Every night, when we went to sleep, we would all climb up the ladder. Then Nimol would throw the ladder down so no one could get down. In the morning he would jump down and put the ladder back up.

Underneath my house there was a hammock tied to the two back stilts. Srey was the only one that used it, and she would relax there with the baby. The baby's name was Kaipiset, and he was really fat.

To the right of my house there was an old bed. We used it as a table, and we ate our meals there. It had a bedspring, but no mattress. Next to the bed there was a big chunk of rock salt. When we needed salt for our food, we would break a piece off and crumble it up. Then we would sprinkle it on our food to flavor it.

In front of the bed a little ways there was a big tree. The tree's trunk was crooked, and it spiraled up toward the branches. I had never seen a tree like this before. The branches of the tree were not twisted like the trunk.

In between the tree and the bed there was a huge black pot and a fireplace for cooking. To the left of my house there were two bushes. One of the bushes produced chile peppers. Srey liked to pick them and use them as a spice for our food. Sometimes she would eat a whole one as a snack. I tried it one time, and I had no idea how hot it would be. I ran across the road to the pump to get some cool water. I could not get enough water to cool my mouth off.

Under one of the bushes I hid a few pieces of broken plates with pretty patterns on them, a couple colorful rocks, and a torn stuffed animal. I hid them there because they were special to me. I hope to some day go back and look for my hidden treasures.

There was a dirt road in front of my house. Across the road there were many other houses, but they were not built on stilts. The jungle was only a few yards behind my house. There were a few small plants here and there, but there was mostly bare dirt between the house and the jungle.

Whenever I got a cut, I would cover it up with sand. I knew that it wasn't good to have an open cut, and I didn't know of any other way to cover it.

Sometimes when I had an earache, Srey would fill my ear with salt water, and I would have to lie down for a few hours. I would usually fall asleep waiting for the water to dry up. When I woke up, I would have a burning sensation in my ear. I didn't like the salt in my ear at all. I would try to brush the salt out with my fingertips. Srey would get mad when she saw me do this. She said the salt was supposed to stay in my ear, and that it would help the pain go away faster. I didn't care because the salt made it hurt worse. She would make me lie down again and put more salt water in my ear. When the water dried up, I would take the salt out again. I made sure she wasn't around when I did this, or she would grab a stick and spank me. I didn't want to be spanked, so I ran away. That didn't help because it made her madder. When she finally caught me, she would spank me hard, but just a few times, so it wasn't that bad.

The water pump was across the road from my house and a little to the left. There were always grownups or kids there. Many of the people in the area used it for washing their clothes, taking baths, and for cooking. Sometimes when it got really hot, all the kids in the area would go there, and we would splash water on each other. It was always so refreshing. Many of the kids took off their clothes and just relaxed there. Sometimes I would see whole families taking baths at the pump. I would see soapsuds everywhere. It wasn't unusual to see people naked. Usually it was small boys who ran around naked. Girls my age didn't do that unless it was extremely hot.

Sometimes I would have to wash clothes by the pump. It was a long process, and I didn't like all that soap on me. The soap had a sticky feeling. I tasted the soapsuds one time. They were awful. Sometimes a little boy would come around and bother me. It made me mad because I hated to wash clothes. Thankfully Srey didn't make me wash everyone's clothes, even though we didn't have that many.

I had two outfits, and I would switch between them every so often. I had two tops and two skirts. Both of my tops were white. My skirts were long and went down to my ankles. They were blue-gray and had a vintage paisley pattern on them.

Srey would always make me fetch some water for her when she needed it for cooking. I had to carry two metal buckets to the pump. Then I would have to pump the handle up and down, and a few seconds later, water would pour out. I didn't mind filling up the buckets, but the part I hated was carrying them across the road. I had to carry a bucket in each hand and slowly walk across the road. I had to be careful not to spill it, or Srey would be upset. Once in a while I had to set the buckets down and rest a minute because they were so heavy.

One time a car was coming down the road, and I had just set my buckets down. Fortunately the car was going slowly. I picked up the buckets and struggled on across. I spilled some water, but I didn't care. At least I was safe.

While I lived at the house on stilts, I made some new friends. There was a girl named Knuu, and she was about a year younger than me. She had an older sister named Kahan. She was about a year older than me. I was about five at the time. There was another girl who hung out with us named Kchrap. She was about two years older than me. She was extremely tall and thin for her age. She could be mean sometimes. She was never mean to me, just to the boys who lived around us. I hung out with these girls a lot, and we played many games together.

Kahan showed me how to jump rope. We would collect rubber bands and tie them together until it was long enough to use as a jump rope. The only bad thing was that the rubber bands were old and would break easily. We could be in the middle of a game of jump rope, and it would break in half. That was no fun. I wasn't too good at jumping rope, so I let the other girls do it.

If none of my friends were around, I would go exploring around the area. There was one tree I found in the jungle that I liked to climb in particular. I remember thinking that I would like to live in that tree some day. Sometimes I would fall asleep in the tree, and I would come home the next morning. My parents wouldn't even notice that I had been gone.

This made me feel sad. I knew that if the baby would suddenly disappear, my parents would panic and go looking for him. I wanted them to be sad and miss me too. It was strange how my parents acted around me. Maybe they hadn't even noticed that I had been gone, or maybe they simply didn't care. They never asked how I was doing or how I felt.

I didn't understand this feeling of belonging that I wanted. Why didn't my parents care about me like they cared about Kaipiset? What I really wanted from my parents more than anything was to be loved, but I didn't even know what love was back then.

Everybody shows love in different ways, and it could be that their way of showing it was by feeding and clothing me. They never showed affection toward me. I never really had a conversation with my parents. I was just there, somehow existing.

There was a place down the road a little ways where a lady in her thirties sold soup packages. She had a small table loaded with tons of them. It was the most I had ever seen. I always wondered where she got all that soup. I started calling her the soup lady because I couldn't remember her name.

Srey sent me to buy from her almost every day. I would try to get a different flavor every time I was there. She soon noticed this, and every time after that, she would hand me a flavor I hadn't tried yet. She was a pleasant lady to talk to. She would ask what I'd been up to, and I would tell her about my friends and what games we played.

Sometimes I would take a walk past where she would be set up, and she wouldn't be there. Soon I noticed that she was only there at a certain time. She only sold from mid-morning to early afternoon. I wondered how she could carry all that soup. She must have lived nearby. I never saw the soup lady put her stuff up or take it down. I often thought that I would some day follow her home or sit with her until she had to leave. Then I could watch her take her stuff away. I never got a chance though. I always had something else on my mind, and when I would remember, she would be gone. The soup lady mystified me.

Whenever my parents went frog hunting, I had to take care of Kaipiset. It was a pretty easy job, except that he would like to run around and go across the road or just stand in the middle of the road. This annoyed me. I had told him many times that it was dangerous to be in the middle of the road. I would chase him everywhere all day long. It got extremely tiring. I could not see how a baby could have so much energy. Kaipiset would laugh every time I was mad at him. He must have had pleasure in seeing me mad.

When Srey came back home, she would have a bucket full of dead frogs. She would turn a frog over on its back, cut it straight down the middle, and take the guts out. After she washed them, she would stuff them with fermented spicy cabbage and other vegetables. Then she would fry them. After showing me what to do, she would have me wash the frogs after she had taken the guts out.

One time Nimol came home with a huge black snake draped around his neck. Its head and tail almost reached the ground. He chopped it up into little pieces and fried some of it. He set the rest of it aside for another meal. That night we had snake pieces and stuffed frog served on top of rice. It was an amazing meal. I liked the vegetables inside the stuffed frog the best. I enjoyed the tender meat of the snake. I probably would have enjoyed it a lot more if it weren't for all the bones. There were still some frogs left over, and we placed them in a container that also held the vegetables. We did that to make the frog meat more tender and give it more flavor.

I had rice every day. In the morning I had a handful of cold cooked rice. For lunch I always had soup, and for dinner I had warm rice served with stir-fried vegetables and some kind of meat.

One afternoon, when I was walking up the road to my house, a big black dog came running toward me. I got scared, and I took off running. The dog was barking viciously, and it was gaining on me. I could hear my heart pounding, and my lungs were screaming for air. My legs ached horribly. As I collapsed by my house, I heard a gunshot go off, and the dog lay dead next to me. Everyone in the neighborhood came to see what all the commotion was about. A young man had shot it and was now examining it. My friends asked me if I was OK.

Some other men came and picked the dog up. I watched where they were carrying it, and they set it on a table across the road. Then one man picked up the biggest knife I had ever seen and started chopping the dog into pieces. He told everyone to come and take a piece of the meat. Srey walked over with a plate, and they gave her two huge slabs of the meat. That was what we had for dinner that night.

The next day I didn't feel so well. I got diarrhea, and I had a bad rash. Srey made me lie in a place by myself so I wouldn't get others sick. The day after that I was fine. For dinner that night we had dog meat again. The next morning the same thing happened. Srey said that I should probably not eat any more dog meat. I was a bit disappointed. I enjoyed it, but I also realized that it was making me sick, and I would rather not be sick. She told me I was allergic to the dog meat.

I went fishing for eels twice. I would dive down about seven or eight feet to the bottom of the river and catch them with my bare hands. The eels swam fast, and I had to hold my breath for a long time. When I ran out of air, I would have to go back to the surface and catch some more air. Then I would go back down again. It was really hard to do. It was exhausting, but it was worth it.

The second time I caught one it shocked me. I didn't know that it was an electric eel, and I didn't expect this. I released it instantly. I opened my mouth to scream, and water entered my lungs. I came up out of the water coughing, and I looked at my hands. They looked all right, but I could feel a vibration in my bones and a tingling sensation in my hands. Then I went back down and caught a different one.

I would take the eels home and fry them myself. I would cut an eel into pieces and put the pieces into a frying pan with some oil. I would cut up some green onions and throw them in with the eel. Then I would heat up some leftover rice, put it on a plate, and place the eel and onions on top of the rice. The eel's meat was tender, and it had a delicate flavor. It was one of my favorite things to eat.

One time while I was walking through the jungle, I saw an elephant. I had never seen one before, but I had heard of them. I was awestruck by its massive size. I could not stop looking at it. A young man was riding it, and he stopped the elephant and told me about it. He asked me if I wanted to ride it. I looked up at him, and he was so high up above me. He jumped down and tried to lift me up onto the elephant. It took a while for me to get up. It didn't help that he was short. At first I kept sliding back down, but I finally managed to get up and gain my balance. I touched its skin. It was rough, and it had creases in it. I couldn't believe how high I was. I was scared and excited all at once.

Then the man nudged the elephant, and it started walking. I felt my stomach go up as the animal began to move. I asked the man if I could get off, so he nudged the elephant to make it stop, and he helped me down. It was a lot easier getting off than getting on. Then the man got back on and rode away. I would never forget that amazing ride.

There was a pond in the jungle where a lot of my friends liked to go swimming. The older kids had races swimming from one side to the other. I always stayed by the edge because I was afraid of deep water. In the middle of the pond there were three wooden posts that stuck out of the water. I didn't know what they were there for, but a lot of my friends liked to linger there.

A girl I knew asked me why I never swam to the middle of the pond. I didn't want to tell her that I was scared, so I started to swim toward her. Suddenly I couldn't feel the bottom beneath me. I started moving my arms and legs frantically, but I wasn't getting anywhere. Instead, I felt myself going down. The water rose above my head, and I started gasping for air. My friend realized that I was struggling, and she grabbed my arm. She helped me reach one of the wooden posts. She asked me if I was all right. I didn't answer. My heart was pounding, and I was still trying to catch my breath. I clung to the wooden post like it was a life preserver. I was afraid that it might disappear, and I would drown. Eventually I gathered the courage and swam back. Somehow I made it across without any problem. Then I got out of the pond and watched the other kids. I never tried to swim across again.

One evening I was walking around an open area in the jungle with A'aom. I called him my older brother, but he wasn't related to me. He was about four years older than me. I was tired, and I sat down. He got out a slingshot and shot it at the sky. I looked up, and he hit a bird with it. He had impressive aim. I was mad at him because I liked birds. He walked a little ways away from me, and when he came back, he had the dead bird in his hand. I asked him why he had killed an innocent bird, and he said that it was food like anything else. We started walking back home, but it got dark before we reached the house, so we stopped. A'aom started a fire and roasted the bird. When it was fully cooked, he asked me if I wanted some. I said no because I felt bad for the bird. I didn't want to watch him eat it, so I went to sleep.

When I awoke the next morning, it was already hot outside. A'aom was nowhere to be found. It didn't bother me much because I knew the jungle, and I could find my way home. I saw a few grasshoppers jumping around, so I sat very still. I caught one and killed it. I did this until I had three of them. The coals from the fire were surprisingly still burning, so I roasted them and ate them. They were nice and crunchy, but some yellow stuff that oozed out didn't taste so good. Then I got up and started walking home.

A minute later I heard A'aom behind me. He called for me to wait for him. I did, and I noticed that he was smoking something. I asked him what it was, and he told me it was a cigarette. I was fascinated with the smoke that came out of his mouth. He asked me if I wanted to try it. He handed it to me, so I placed it in my mouth and sucked in. Smoke filled my lungs, and I spat it out. I started coughing violently, and A'aom started laughing. I had not expected that to happen. I got mad at him and ran the rest of the way home.

I was always fascinated by all the vehicles that passed by my house. One day I saw a tank driving down the road. It was the largest thing I had ever seen. It had metal treads that were longer than the rest of the tank. There was a young man sitting at the opening on the top. The tank slowed to a stop, and he asked if I wanted to ride up there with him. I was excited and said that I did. I somehow managed to climb up, and he sat me on his lap. He looked different from anyone I had ever seen. He was light complected, but he had a tan like he had been out in the sun a lot. He didn't look like anyone in the village. He was probably American or French. He said that I was the prettiest little girl that he had ever seen.

Then the tank started to move slowly. I hadn't noticed that it had moved until I realized that I wasn't in front of my house any more. I got scared, and I didn't want this young man to take me away. I jumped off his lap and landed on the ground hard. The young man looked frightened and told me what I had just done was very dangerous. He said I shouldn't have jumped while the tank was moving. The tank could have crushed me. The tank stopped when I jumped off. I reached over, touched the tank's tread, and felt its sharp rough pattern. The young man told me that that was dangerous, so I stepped back. He said that when he came back on this road he would look for me and see how I was doing, but I never saw him again.

Sometimes if it got really hot I would sit under my house. It was nice and cool in the shade. Srey would rest on the hammock with Kaipiset and breast-feed him. During these times I would look out across from my house and wonder what the road led to. I often heard gunshots up the road, but it wouldn't bother me unless they were loud, or if there were a lot of them going off at once. I always wondered why there were so many. I heard them almost every day.

Every morning, right before I woke up, a rooster would crow. It was like a wakeup call, but it would be annoying whenever I wanted more sleep. It seemed like it would never stop crowing until I actually got up. It was like it knew that I wasn't up yet. The rooster belonged to one of my neighbors.

One evening Srey was about to make dinner. She cooked the rice and vegetables while Nimol went fishing. At least that's how it usually was. Sometimes Nimol would say he was going fishing, but he would come back without any fish. When he came home, he would act really strange.

One time Nimol said that he was going to go fishing. He picked up the fishing nets and took off as usual, but for some reason I had a feeling there was something else going on. I quietly followed him.

A little ways into the jungle he started going in a different direction. He never turned around, so I knew that it was safe to follow him. Suddenly, as I looked ahead, I saw a fire and heard a group of men laughing. Nimol joined them. I hid behind a few bushes only a few feet away. As I watched, he picked up a bottle and started to drink. I knew exactly what was happening.

Then he noticed me. His smile vanished, and his eyes narrowed. He looked mean and stern as he glared at me. The look he gave me was like he wanted to kill me. It scared me, and I ran all the way back home. I didn't tell Srey about anything that I had seen. I ate my rice and vegetables that evening, but without fish this time. It took me a long time to get to sleep. I would never forget that look he gave me.

When I woke up the next morning, I found Srey and Nimol snuggling with each other. Nimol must have returned in the middle of the night or early in the morning. When they were awake, he acted like nothing had ever happened. That afternoon, after Srey and the baby had gone somewhere, Nimol walked up to me. He grabbed me by the hair and told me that if he ever saw me follow him again, he would kill me. He flung me to the ground, kicked me a few times, and left. I cried for fear that I was going to die.

That was probably the most Nimol had ever said to me at any time. I never thought he ever loved me. He hardly ever spoke to me kindly.

A few evenings later, Nimol hadn't come back for a long time. He was supposed to be fishing. While I was cleaning up, I heard a shuffling noise. I looked up to see Nimol. He started yelling at me angrily. I noticed that he had an axe in his hand. Srey jumped up and grabbed the baby. She took off running and screamed for me to run too. I dropped everything and took off.

Nimol came after me, and I ran across the road. Clouds covered the sky, and I couldn't see anything in the darkness. I ran into a bush and fell. Then a hand grabbed me. I was about to scream, but another hand covered my mouth as I was dragged behind the bush. I looked up to see Srey. She motioned for me to be quiet. I heard Nimol's footsteps walk right past us. He paused for a second, and I held my breath. Then he walked back home. I was relieved that he hadn't spotted us. That night we slept under the bush.

The next morning we went back home. Nimol asked us where we had been. He had forgotten what had happened the night before. It seemed strange that he could forget doing something like that. Srey told him exactly what had happened that night. He told her that he was sorry and didn't remember any of it, but I didn't believe him.

Three nights later it happened again. He came home drunk, and he was really mad at me. He had the axe in his hand, and in a rage he swung it at me. He missed me by inches, and the axe flew out of his hand. That made him even madder, and he went to pick up the axe. I started running, trying to find a place to hide. I stumbled and fell, and I hit my face on a rock. I could feel a loose tooth in my mouth, and I tasted blood. There was a pain in my foot, and I couldn't get up. I turned over and saw Nimol coming with the axe again. Everything seemed to be happening in slow motion. As he aimed the axe at me, I closed my eyes. Suddenly, out of nowhere, I felt a pair of hands on my shoulders. Then everything went black.

The next day I found myself lying down, and there were two ladies looking at me with worried expressions. At first I wondered who they were. I had an awful headache. Then I recalled what had happened the night before. I had fallen and hit my head. One of the ladies was my neighbor, and she had saved my life. The other lady, I realized, was Srey. I thanked my neighbor for saving me. I later found out that I had broken my left pinky toe.

When Srey and I went back home, Nimol asked Srey where we had been. She told him exactly what had happened that night. Once again he did not recall ever doing such a thing. I thought it was strange that Srey would tell Nimol exactly where we hid from him because then he could find us and hurt us.

Nimol kept chasing me with the axe for a while. It didn't happen every day, and sometimes not even for weeks. Then without warning it would happen again. I never knew when to expect it, and I was scared every night. We hid at our neighbors' house every time it happened, but strangely, Nimol could never find us, even after Srey had told him where we had been. It was like he had a split personality and forgot everything. I was thankful for that.

I was afraid of any sharp object from then on. For a while I was afraid to cut my own food. Srey wondered why Nimol was so mad at me. I explained to her what I had seen, but she thought I was lying. She found a stick and spanked me with it. She told me that I shouldn't make up stories about my dad. I ran away crying. I knew I had told the truth, but no matter how much I tried to convince her, she wouldn't believe me. I never told her about Nimol hurting me because I knew she would spank me again. I wanted so bad just to tell someone who would believe me, but there was no one.

I had two cousins named Bongno and Bongnan. I called them my cousins, but they weren't related to me. Bongno was about seventeen, and Bongnan was about fifteen. They were sisters, and they looked almost identical. They could have been twins except that Bongno was a little taller. They lived in a cement house about a mile away. It was the biggest house I had seen so far.

Across from their house there was a man who had a lot of pigs. The pigs ran loose everywhere in his yard. I always saw him working outside tending to the pigs. Usually I saw him feeding them. He had a bucket full of thick gray mush that he would dump into a trough, and all the little pigs would scramble to eat it.

Next to his place, a few yards to the right, there was a little restaurant. It was the only restaurant I had ever seen. I had only been there once. I was walking past the restaurant, and a lady came out and asked me if I was hungry. I told her that I was, and she invited me inside. I sat down at a table, and she handed me a bowl. I was about to use my fingers to eat when she handed me a fork. I had never seen or used one before, but I figured out how to use it right away. In the bowl was some spaghetti-like food with meatballs. Most of the meat I ate came from the river, so it was a great treat.

One day Srey sent me to see Bongno and Bongnan. When I walked into their yard, they came outside. We talked for a while around a cement fountain in front of their house. I played with the leaves that had fallen on it. I threw some leaves at them, and they threw a few back.

Then they asked me if I wanted to take a walk, and I said yes. We walked to the left side of their house and out back a few yards. We came up to some fence posts and walked around them. I looked around, and all I could see was fields of dirt. I asked them about it, and they said that this was their farm, but nothing was being grown at the moment. We walked along the edge of the field for a very long time, and then I started to see plants. I looked around and realized that this place seemed familiar. We had reached my family's farm. I couldn't believe that we had walked that far. We were getting tired, so we decided to walk back to their house.

When we got back, their grandmother was sitting outside on the porch. She saw me and went inside. She came back a minute later carrying a container full of shrimp. She told me to give it to Srey. I left their house, and as I was walking past some bushes that grew in front of my cousins' place, I ate a few shrimp. They were delicious.

I wasn't watching where I was going. I tripped over my own feet, and the shrimp went flying. Most of the shrimp had fallen and had gotten dirty. I picked them up, knowing that they couldn't be eaten. I put all the shrimp back in the container and stood there for a moment, wondering what to do with the dirty shrimp. There were some bushes beside me, and that gave me an idea. I hid the container in the branches of one of the bushes. I made sure that no one would be able to see it. I was happy that I had found a solution and thought to myself, now that problem is fixed. I never did tell Srey about the shrimp.

I continued past the place where the man had the pigs. I noticed that he was cutting the stems off of some banana leaves. There were tons of them lying around. He was using the stems to make food for the pigs. I asked him if the pigs actually liked them. At this question, he laughed and said that they did. I asked him if I could take a few leaves. He told me that I could, and he went back to work.

I walked back home dragging the banana leaves, wondering what I could use them for. I was almost home when a little boy came up to me and asked what I was doing. I told him that the banana leaves looked neat, and that I wasn't sure what I was going to do with them yet.

Suddenly an idea came to my head. I told the boy to sit on the banana leaf, and he did. Then I pulled the leaf, dragging him along with me. He was having a great time. He wanted me to go faster. Some other kids came along and asked what I was doing. They all wanted to ride the banana leaf too. I gave the boy another banana leaf, and he pulled his friend.

Ever since that, my friends and I would go see the man with the pigs and ask for banana leaves. He asked me what I was using them for, and when I told him, he laughed. Since he only used the stems to feed the pigs, he said that I could take as many as I wanted. All my friends loved this game, especially Knuu, because she was small and easy to drag. I would drag her as fast as I could, and she loved it. The only

29

bad thing about the banana leaves was that they would wear out from being dragged so much. Then we couldn't use them any more, and we would have to get a new one.

I would sometimes walk past the bushes and see if the container of shrimp was still there. A few days later, when I opened the container, the shrimp had dried up. I thought this was strange. I wondered what had caused that to happen. I ate one to see how it tasted. It was no good. It was hard and had no flavor. I was disappointed.

There was a path in the jungle that I liked to follow. It had some smooth rocks here and there. They felt good under my feet, and I liked to walk on them. I wasn't sure how the rocks got there, but they led to the river.

One night I followed this path through the darkness. I walked over the rocks and felt my way through the jungle. When I got to the river, there was a boat waiting for me. Nimol was in the boat, and he told me to hurry and get in. He rowed us across the river, and when we had almost reached the other side, he pushed me off the boat and told me to find someone. I swam the rest of the way across. I wondered, who in the world could he be talking about? I walked into the trees until I could hardly see anything. It was a moonless night, and the darkest I had ever seen. For a while I thought I was dreaming. Then I heard a noise, and a girl came over to me. I couldn't see her face, but by her height I could tell she was older than me, but not yet an adult. She had very long hair. She told me something, but I couldn't remember what she said.

Then I ran back to the river. The boat was gone, and Nimol was nowhere in sight, so I swam back across. It was very difficult because the current was strong. I was so exhausted that I almost gave up. I almost let the river take me, but the girl was still there at the edge of the river and told me to keep swimming. I used the last of my strength, and somehow I managed to get across. When I looked back, the girl was gone. I thought to myself, how strange! She was there one minute and gone the next. I started back into the jungle and felt my way home. By then there were some stars out that provided some light, and I could see a little better.

I woke up the next morning extremely sore. I wondered why, and then I recalled what had happened the night before. It all seemed like a dream, but I wasn't sure. Nimol didn't say anything to me the next morning. There was still something that bothered me about what had happened. The girl had told me something. She had said that it was extremely important, yet no matter how hard I tried, I couldn't remember any of it.

That evening Nimol came home and told Srey that something wasn't right about his boat. He seemed confused. It made me wonder if my experience that night really wasn't a dream.

One afternoon Srey told me to go to the bank and get her some money. She said that I could use some of the money to buy ice cream. I was excited because I had heard of it, but I had never had it before. Bongno and Bongnan came with me.

It was a long walk to the bank. The bank was a small room in a cement building. We walked over to a man sitting at the window, and I asked him if I could have some money. I'd been to the bank before, and he knew me, so he handed me some money. I gave it to my cousin, and we went looking for a place that sold ice cream.

We found a young man selling ice cream from a metal cart. I asked him for three ice creams, one for me and the other two for Bongno and Bongnan. He opened a metal container, and he took out a bread roll and a scoop. Then he put two scoops of ice cream into the bread roll to make an ice cream sandwich. He gave it to me, and he made two more. The ice cream tasted so good. It was very sweet, but not as sweet as sugar cane. The ice cream helped to cool us off from the long walk in the hot sun. When I finished it, I wanted another one. Bongno told me that I couldn't have any more because she didn't want me to waste the money.

She said that Srey would be upset if all the money had been spent on ice cream. It was a luxury, and since my parents didn't have that much money, we could only get it once. When we arrived home, Bongno gave Srey the money. I told Srey about how amazing the ice cream was, and she just smiled.

Farming

ការធ្វើស្រែចំការ

Sometimes I would run through the cornfields with my arms outstretched, pretending that I could fly. I could feel the rough leaves pass through my fingers. I liked running through the cornfields. They were like an endless maze. When I looked up, it amazed me how tall those plants were. They were taller than my parents.

I met a girl who was close to my age when her parents came to help us out with the farming. We liked to play hide and seek in the cornfields. I would turn around, and she would take off in the opposite direction. Then she would call out for me to find her. I would listen to where her voice came from and walk in that direction. I was very good at this game because I could catch the slightest movement and sound. When I knew I was close, I would lie down quietly on my stomach and look for her between the cornstalks. If I didn't see her in one direction, I would look in the other. When I saw her legs, I would crawl up close to her. It was funny to see her standing still, listening for me. It was hard to keep from laughing out loud. I was right next to her, and she didn't even know it. I would reach over and grab her ankle, and she would scream. I would then get up and tell her that I had found her. Then it would be her turn. She wasn't so good at this game because she made a lot of noise. I would be nice and let her catch me, or the game would go on forever if I stayed quiet.

Only once did I ever get scared while I was out in the cornfields. I was having fun playing, and I didn't realize how late it had gotten. It was very dark by then. I tried to find my way out, but I couldn't tell where I was going. I felt like a blind person, all alone in the world. I crashed into cornstalks wherever I turned. I started yelling for help, but no one was there. I listened, but I couldn't hear anyone. All I heard was insects. I figured out that my parents had already gone home. I walked a little farther, and I started crying because I knew I was lost. It was so dark that I could feel it on my skin. I didn't like this feeling of being alone. I was determined to get out. I knew that corn grew in straight rows, so I tried to keep between the rows to walk in as straight a line as possible. I knew that if I walked straight, I would eventually get out. I walked for what seemed like hours, but I finally found my way out. I was so tired and relieved when I got out that I collapsed on the ground and fell asleep. I woke up the next morning. It was a long walk back home. My parents hadn't even noticed that I had been gone.

Sometimes I would help my parents with the farming. My favorite thing to do was plant rice. The rice paddy would be mushy mud, and it felt good as it squished between my toes. I would have to pick up the rice plants from where they were and replant them in another place. I didn't know why this had to be done. I guessed that it was to help the rice grow better.

Sometimes Srey would make me go to a place where the mud was really mushy. The mud went up to the middle of my thighs, and I could easily walk through it as if I was wading through water. Srey would make me look for crabs in the mud. I would have to stick my arms down into the mud and feel around for the crabs. I was pretty good at finding them. I would have to be careful because I didn't want to get pinched by them. Once I found one, I would place it in a basket. The crabs weren't that big, but if I caught enough, they would be good for one meal.

I remember finding a big crab one time. I was wading through the mud to place the crab in the basket when suddenly I felt a sharp pain in my left big toe. I walked faster to the edge of the field and threw the big crab in the basket. I lifted my foot, and attached to it was another crab. Srey saw this and burst into laughter. I tried to pull it off, but it wouldn't budge. I tried to kick it off, but that didn't work either. Then I sat down and started kicking my leg up and down trying to get the crab off. Seeing this, Srey laughed even harder. She didn't even try to take the crab off, so I tried to pry it off with my fingers. I was getting really frustrated. I was about to give up when it finally let go. I was mad at the crab, and I flung it to the ground. Then I threw it in the basket with the other crabs. After that, I didn't feel like going back into the mud to look for more. I looked at Srey, and she was planting rice again as if nothing had happened. Then I went off looking for something else to do. The mud eventually dried out on my skin, and I rubbed it off.

My second favorite thing to do was to cut the corn with a sickle. I would have to get down close to the ground and chop the cornstalk. Then I would lay it in a pile with the others. When I got tired of that, or when Srey asked me to help her, I would take the cornstalks and yank the ears off. Then I would place the ears in a basket. I never got to go with my parents to see where it was taken.

All of the crops came in about the same time. When the rice was due to be harvested, I had to use a sickle. It would cut through the rice plant easily, and I liked how it felt to grab a bundle of rice and chop through it. It amazed me how the rice could be cut so easily with the sickle. I would have to get a single rice plant to tie the bundle together. Then I would stack the bundles in a pile. The process was fast, and I enjoyed it.

My parents would take the rice to another farm where they sold it. I remember going to that farm one time. There was a large building that looked like a barn. In front of it, there was the biggest pile of rice plants I had ever seen. It was about four or five feet high. Outside, there were people hitting the rice plants on the ground. They were trying to get the rice off the plants. Then they would throw the rice into the air, and the black coating that covered the rice grains would fall off.

While my parents talked to the owner of the farm, I went to explore the area. I saw an old tree and walked over to it. When I reached it, I almost fell into a ditch that was right behind the tree. The ditch stretched out as far as I could see. I walked down into it, wondering what it was used for.

When I looked up toward the tree, I hadn't realized how far down I was. I got a little scared and started climbing back up. It wasn't as easy going up as it was to go down. I would get so far up, and all of a sudden the dirt beneath me would come loose, and I would slide backwards. It was really hot outside that day, and it made me sweat a lot. I started climbing back up more carefully, and I eventually got out of the ditch. Srey rushed over and asked me where I had been. When I told her, she was upset because she had called for me, and I hadn't come. Then we walked back home with Nimol.

When it was time to pick the onions, I would dig down into the ground with my fingers to pull them out. I would have to pull the whole plant out, including the roots. I would then place them in a basket, and Srey would take them to the market to sell. I was never allowed to go to the market with her.

Working on the farm was a lot of fun, but I didn't farm that much. Most of the time I would run around and play with other kids that happened to come past the farm.

School

សាលារៀន

One afternoon I was sitting under my house enjoying the shade. I looked across the road and saw a table set up close to the water pump. There were a lot of grownups around it. Both of my parents were there too, which surprised me, because Nimol would almost never be around during the daytime. I was curious about what was going on, so I walked across the road over to where they were. There were two people standing behind the table, and they were writing something down on a paper. I didn't get to look long because Srey grabbed my arm and told me that we were going back home. She told me that I would be going to school. I looked at her and asked her what school was. She didn't answer my question. She just told me that in the morning I would go. That evening Nimol handed me a board and a white stick. I asked him what they were, but he didn't answer.

That night I couldn't sleep, and the next morning I got up early. I had wondered all night what school was. I hoped that it was a nice place. I was surprised to see that my parents were already up. I climbed down the ladder and saw Srey. She saw me, and she told me to come and eat. She put a handful of rice in my left hand and the board with the white stick in my right hand. She said that I was going to school. I thought, so early! She walked me over to the road. Then she pointed down the road and told me to follow it until I got to a bridge. She said that to the left of the bridge I would see a white building, and that would be the school. She told me to start walking. I wondered why she didn't come with me.

I walked slowly, and I looked around at my surroundings. I saw some things that I hadn't noticed before. There was a cornfield next to my neighbors' house. I hadn't realized how pretty it looked. I looked down and realized that I was still carrying the rice in my hand. I wasn't hungry, so I threw it into the cornfield. I turned around and looked back at my house, and Srey wasn't there any more. I was unsure of what to do. I looked at the corn and touched the leaves on it. I closed my eyes and sighed. Then I turned around and started walking toward the school. I remembered the directions that Srey had given me, and ran through them over and over again in my mind. I didn't want to get lost. I wondered how far away this school was. I walked for what seemed like five miles. By then I was very tired. After passing our farm, all I saw was trees, and they went on forever. I started thinking that I was lost. I had never walked so far down this road before. I hadn't come to the bridge yet, but I kept on walking. I was sweating so much that my hair felt like someone had dipped it in water. I was getting really thirsty. I felt so alone. Not a single car had passed by while I was walking.

Then I saw it. There was the bridge. I thought I was never going to find it. I looked to the left, but I saw no sign of a school. I walked further, and still I did not see it. I retraced my steps. I stopped and thought about Srey's directions again. That's when I heard kids laughing. I followed the noise and found a dirt path I hadn't noticed before. There were so many trees around that it was hard to see. I followed it, and it brought me to an open area. There was a building to the right, and on top of a little hill nearby there was another building. There were kids everywhere. I was relieved to have found the school.

I walked over to the building on the right and looked inside. There was an opening for a door and a huge square gap in the wall. It was supposed to be a window, but there was no glass in it. There were desks on both sides of the room, and there was a narrow aisle in the middle. They were like long narrow tables that had benches connected to them. The benches had no backs. There was room for five kids to sit at each desk. Each desk was pressed up against the one in front of it. The desks filled most of the room. Later, I noticed that there was a chalkboard that stretched out across the front wall.

Then someone grabbed my arm, and I turned around. It was A'aom. He had a huge grin, and he said that I would like school. I asked him what the board and white stick were. He told me that they were a chalkboard and chalk. He said that we used them to write. Then all the kids rushed toward the door and went to their seats. After that, A'aom left me.

I was the last one to come in. The *ne' kruu* (teacher) saw me and asked me what my name was. All the kids looked at me. I felt nervous and shy. He walked me to my seat. His name was Sawk, and I learned that he was my teacher. I noticed that the younger kids sat in the front and the older ones in the back. There were about thirty kids in the class.

Ne' Kruu Sawk told the kids my age to write our names; he told the students in the other grades to do something different. I had never written my name before. I looked at the other kids in my row. They picked up their chalk and started writing. The kids then turned their chalkboards over and put one hand on the desk, palm up. I didn't know what to do, so I scribbled on the board. I turned it over and put my hand facing up like the rest of the students. *Ne' Kruu* Sawk walked to the first student in my row. He turned over that student's chalkboard and looked at what had been written. He would go to each student and do the same thing. I noticed that as he passed them, they would each turn their hand over.

Then he came to me. He picked up my board and looked at it. I looked up at him, and he had no expression on his face. He had a long thin stick in his hand that I hadn't noticed before. He slapped the palm of my hand with it. It didn't hurt, but I was taken by surprise. I had not expected that to happen, and I didn't understand what that meant. None of the kids so far had gotten their hand slapped. When he got to the last kid in the row, he slapped his hand too. I thought to myself, at least I wasn't the only one. Then the teacher went to the next row and checked their chalkboards. When he got back to the front of the room, he asked the boy who had gotten his hand slapped to sit next to me. The boy looked nervous, and the rest of the kids scooted down to give him room. The teacher talked about other stuff for the rest of the school day.

School was about three hours long. The older kids got to leave first. We left in single file. We waited for the rows behind us to leave until it was our row's turn. My row was the last to leave. The teacher was standing by the door. The students would stop, put their hands together, and bow their head as they passed him. The teacher would stand there and look at each student. I had seen this done once before, when I had gone to see the *proh ong*. I knew that it was a sign of respect. When it was my turn, I put my hands together and looked up at the teacher. He looked down at me, smiled, put his hands together, and bowed his head. He was trying to show me what to do. I realized that, and bowed my head. I felt ashamed. I felt like I had done nothing right that day.

I walked outside and started to walk back home. A girl who sat in my row came up to me and asked me what my name was. She picked up a stick and wrote it in the dirt. I traced over it. She told me to practice. I asked her why *Ne' Kruu* Sawk had slapped my hand. She said it was to tell me that I had gotten my answer wrong.

When I got home that day, I was starving. I realized that I shouldn't have thrown the rice away that Srey had given me before school. She gave me some soup, and that helped me feel a lot better. I was so tired from the long walk in the hot sun. I slept well that night.

The school was built at the edge of the jungle. All the buildings were white. In my building there were two classrooms. My room held kids from five to ten years of age. Next to my room there was a room full of younger kids. They ranged from ages three to four. There was another building a few yards away that faced my building. That building held kids eleven years of age and older. In between these two buildings there was an open space where all the kids played. There was another old building at the end of the play area to the left. It was not being used at the time. The three buildings formed a U shape around the play area. In the right corner, next to my building, there was a water fountain. There were trees all around the school. It was a beautiful area.

The next day it was the same routine. At least I knew what to expect, but when I arrived at school, I realized that I hadn't brought my chalkboard and chalk. I knew I couldn't walk all the way back home for it. I thought, oh great. I didn't want my day to turn out bad like the day before.

Then the girl who had talked to me the day before came over and gave me a stick. She told me to practice writing my name. She showed me how, and I would copy. She was very nice and supportive.

School was about to start when I spotted Bongno and Bongnan. They were my favorite girls. I shouted to them, and they waved and smiled. They were just about to go inside the building on the hill. Then I noticed that the kids from my class were going inside, and I rushed toward the group by the door. Once again all the students put their hands together and bowed their heads. This time I did it right as I passed by my teacher. I walked over to my seat, and I found my chalkboard and chalk still sitting on top of the desk. I had forgotten them and left them there the day before.

I took my seat, and *Ne' Kruu* Sawk asked the two of us that had gotten our names wrong the day before to write our names again. He then started assigning other things to the rest of the class. I started to write my name, but I forgot a letter. My friend noticed this. She whispered something to the boy next to her, and he whispered something to the girl next to him. That girl grabbed my chalkboard and handed it down to my friend. She put my chalkboard on her lap so the teacher couldn't see it, and she wrote something. She passed it down, and it was handed back to me. I looked at it, and she had written my name for me. I remembered the letter that I had forgotten. I erased what she had written and wrote it over. Then I turned my chalkboard over and put my hand facing up. *Ne' Kruu* Sawk started at the first desk and started going down the row. When he came to me, I was

45

nervous. He picked up my chalkboard and paused for a second in surprise. I looked up at him, and he smiled. He moved on to the boy who had also gotten his name wrong last time and checked his chalkboard. He then slapped the boy's hand again. I felt sorry for him. No one had bothered to help teach him.

After going to school for about a week, Srey told me that I was supposed to walk with another girl about my age. I walked with her, but we didn't have much to say to each other. She was new to our neighborhood. When we arrived at school, I was surprised to see no other kids outside. I knew I was late, so I ran to the door and walked inside. The other girl followed me. All the students' eyes turned to us. It felt like it was the first day of school again. The teacher looked upset. He told us to stand by the chalkboard. He said that as a punishment for being late we would have to stand on one foot for the rest of the school day. We stood facing the class. He said that we could not look down, and if we lost our balance, we would have to do it all over again the next day. I did not want to stand for any longer than I had to. My legs began to ache. I was thankful that I had a good sense of balance because I knew that if I didn't, I couldn't have stood there for three hours. I didn't want to do it again, and that made me more determined not to fall. Time passed by so slowly, and my leg fell asleep. I did not like the tingly feeling, and I wanted to move. It felt like ants crawling up my leg. It was absolute torture.

The new girl cried, but she somehow managed to keep her balance. I did not like being the center of attention. I never had so many eyes looking at me as if they were saying that I was a bad person. I was never late to school again. I never saw any other student late either. The new girl hated school from the beginning. This did not surprise me because of what had happened to us. She refused to go some days. I didn't want to be late again, so I would leave without her. It made me feel bad to do that.

One of the things I learned about was a place called America, where there were buildings made out of gold. *Ne'* *Kruu* Sawk mentioned that everyone there was rich, and they could spend money on anything they wanted. America sounded strange to me. I didn't see what they would need all that money for. He asked if any of us would ever want to go there. I thought about it, but I said no because I liked where I was.

On the way to school, I liked to look around at my surroundings to see if there was anything interesting. There was a small pond across the road from my family's farm. I liked to look at the lily pads that grew in the pond. I was fascinated by how big they were, and wondered how they could float on the water. Their flowers were beautiful. Sometimes I would even see small frogs jumping about. I wanted to stop and catch them, but I was afraid that I would lose track of time and arrive late at school. I didn't want to stand on one foot for three hours again.

One time while I was on my way to school, I saw some men standing outside around a table. They had long sticks, and they would take turns hitting the ends of them against some balls on the table. I was curious about what they were doing, so I watched for a while. One man would take his stick, position it close to his eyes, and hit a white ball. Suddenly more balls were rolling all over the table. Some of them even disappeared. I was taken by surprise when I saw this. Then I realized that I had been there too long, so I started walking again.

When school ended that day, I saw the table again. I walked over to it, and I figured out where the balls had gone. There were holes at the edge of each side of the table, and that's where they had fallen. I hoped to some day come and play that game, but I never got a chance. The next day when I passed by the place where the table was, it was gone. I was a bit upset. I wondered what had happened to the table and why it had disappeared so fast.

After school one day, Bongno and Bongnan asked me if I wanted to visit one of my friends. I said I did, and they took me to the place where my bamboo house used to be. The remains of my old house were no longer there. I wondered what had happened to it. I got to see the girl who was my neighbor. We stayed the night at her house.

The next morning, we had to go to school. On the way, we had to walk through the jungle, and I ran ahead of Bongno and Bongnan. We had to wade through the river on the way to school. I didn't expect the current to be so strong. I started to walk across, and I couldn't move. All of a sudden a gush of water surged toward me. I fell backwards, and my face was under the water. I thought I was going to drown. I tried to get up, but I couldn't. I opened my mouth in a panic, and water rushed into my lungs. Then a hand grabbed me. When I came up out of the water I was coughing and sputtering. My lungs burned from all the water going down while air was trying to come out at the same time. It was Bongno who had saved me. She was stronger, and the current didn't pull her down. She helped me to cross the rest of the way. She was a little upset with me. She had told me to wait for her, but I was excited to get to school and had run ahead. I learned not to do that again. It was sort of refreshing to be wet though because it was so hot. By the time we reached the school, my clothes were dry.

Along the way I talked about the long walk to school from my house. Bongno told me that I lived farther from school than any of the other kids. I was surprised to hear that. Bongno told me that it was the closest school in the area. I had no idea that there were other schools around.

One day A'aom had run out of chalk. After school he asked me if I wanted to go with him to buy some more. I didn't have anything else to do, so I went with him. We walked about half a mile past the school and came to a small shop. There was a young man there. A'aom asked him for some chalk, and the man gave him a whole pack that contained about five pieces.

I had never been this far before, and I looked around. There were so many other shops. I noticed that the road was actually paved here. It was the first time that I had seen a paved road. There were a lot of cars on the road. I contemplated about that place for a while. I came to the conclusion that this place must be where all the cars came from. I wanted to walk farther to see what else there was. A'aom said no. He told me it was dangerous, but he didn't say why. I was a little upset, but he handed me a pack of chalk too. This made me happy. We then walked homeward.

About half way home A'aom disappeared. I looked around, but I couldn't see him anywhere. I wasn't too worried, so I kept on walking. Soon I came to my family's farm. My parents were there, and they were about to leave. Our horse was there too. It was a pretty white horse. I had never paid attention to the horse before, but this time my parents let me ride it. I loved this because I liked being up high. It felt good to not have to walk the rest of the way back home. It was the only time that I got to ride the horse.

Sometimes after school there would be a table outside with food on it. One time when Bongno and Bongnan were outside waiting for me, Bongno bought me a soft clear cube that had coconut inside it. The food wobbled in my hand. I couldn't believe food could move like that. It was something like jello. Bongno and Bongnan laughed because I was so amazed at how it seemed to move by itself. I only remember getting it once. It was delicious, and I begged Bongno and Bongnan for more. They said that they didn't have any more money, so they couldn't get me any more.

Going Away

ទៅឆ្ងាយ

One day about the middle of the afternoon, Srey told me to take a bath. I thought this was strange because I had never been told to do that before. I'd always done that on my own. She handed me a pretty white dress, and she told me to put it on when I was done. I went and took a bath at the pump, and then I came back home. Srey put lipstick on me and brushed my hair. She had never tended to my hair before. I knew that something strange was going on.

A few minutes later I saw a motorcycle coming toward our house. A middle-aged man stepped off the motorcycle and walked over to Srey. They started talking, but I didn't understand what was happening. Nimol came too, and he started talking with them. This was very unusual because I would rarely see Nimol during the daytime. The next thing I knew, I was being placed on the motorcycle, and this strange man was taking me away. My parents didn't do anything about it.

As he started the motorcycle, I looked back. I saw Nimol standing next to Srey and the baby. I looked at the house on stilts. Then I looked to my right, and I saw some of my friends stop playing. They all watched with curious eyes. They were probably wondering what was going on and where I was going. I was thinking that too. I had a strange feeling that I wouldn't be coming back to my house on stilts. I looked back at Srey, and she didn't even say goodbye or cry. She just stood there with no expression on her face. Then I looked at Nimol, and for once in my life I actually felt that he might be kind of sad that I was leaving. Maybe he did care a little bit about me because if he didn't care, he probably wouldn't have come to see me one last time. Or, maybe he was happy to see me go. I would never know. When I saw him turn and walk away, he started chopping some wood, of course with the same axe that he had chased me with. I didn't want my last memory to be of him, so I looked away.

As the motorcycle sped up, everything around me started going by really fast. It made me feel a little sick, so I turned and looked forward. This made me feel better because it made things seem like they weren't going by as fast. Thoughts were running through my head about where I was going and who this stranger was that I was riding with. We passed many houses, and I saw new places that I had never seen before. I noticed that the houses were closer together like a neighborhood.

Then the motorcycle turned left, slowed down, and we came to a house. It belonged to the man on the motorcycle. A couple of other men came out and started talking with him. He asked me if I was hungry, and I said no. I was actually starving, but I didn't want him to know that. His wife came out of the house, gave me a hug, and said a lot of nice things about me. He told her to get something to wipe my lipstick off. She came back a minute later with a wet towel. She gave it to him, and he wiped it off. He said that he didn't like it, and that I looked better without it. Then we got on the motorcycle again, and I was on it for another hour.

Seinique

ស្រីណិក

The man on the motorcycle stopped in front of a large white house. A short lady opened the door and greeted him. She seemed extremely nice. A girl who was a couple years older than me came over and stood next to her. She was the prettiest girl I had ever seen. She had sky blue eyes and brownish blond hair that went down to her waist. Then the man on the motorcycle set me down and started the motorcycle up. Before he left, he gave me some money. He smiled and drove off, and the nice lady went inside. Then the girl started saying mean things to me, and she pushed me down. I had no idea why. The nice lady came back outside and saw what she had done. She scolded her in a language I didn't understand. After that, she told the girl to show me around the neighborhood.

Then the girl smiled and was nice to me. She took me by the hand, and we walked across the street. There was a little boy sitting in a tire swing. The girl said that she wasn't friends with him any more because she had a new friend. She pushed him off the swing. He started to cry, and she walked away. I felt bad for him. I wasn't sure of what to do or say, so I followed her.

We came to an ice cream cart, and since I had money, I bought an ice cream cone for her and one for me. Then we walked over to a grassy area where there were some machines that made a continuous humming sound. We sat on one of them, and the girl talked about what she liked, and about school. She told me that her name was Seinique, and that she was half French and half Cambodian. I found out that the nice lady was her mother, and that her name was Ma' Lee. We talked for a long time, and we became best friends. Every time we finished our ice cream, we would go back and get another one. By the time my money was almost gone, I had bought three ice cream cones for each of us.

When we were almost done eating, Seinique walked me back to her house. On the way I met one of her friends. Her friend was inside her house, and she poked her head out the window as we walked by. She had brown hair and a light skin tone. The girl asked me if I wanted a comb. I took the comb and thanked her. Then I gave her the rest of my money. I don't know why I did this. The girl was so surprised and excited about this that she left the window and walked out of the room. Seinique walked me the rest of the way to her house. She said that I shouldn't just give money away like that.

When we went inside, it was not what I had expected. The floor was not dirt, but cement. It was a big house, and it was spotlessly clean. Seinique took me to the left into a room, and there was a large structure in the middle of the room with a see-through cloth hanging down over it. It was a pretty sight. I wondered what it was. Seinique told me that it was a bed, and that's where people slept. We walked over to it, and I touched it. It was the softest thing I had ever felt.

We walked out of the room, down the hallway, and turned right into another room. Two boys were sitting there. They were beautiful, and they smiled at me. They were about sixteen and seventeen years old. They both had black hair. One had green eyes, and the other had blue eyes. I had never seen anyone like this before. They left the room, and Seinique told me that they were her brothers.

I noticed a large reed mat on the floor. Seinique said that this was where they ate. We walked back into the hallway, and she opened another door. This surprised me. I had never seen a house that had two doors. When we got outside, she told me that this was the place where I could *chu-nóm*. It was a small grassy area, and there was a square cement block in the middle of it. I wondered why it was there. It seemed out of place. I looked out across the yard, and I could see the backs of other houses, but they were much smaller than hers. Seinique's house was on top of a slope, so it was more like looking down onto her neighbors' houses. We walked around the house and back to the front door. We talked there for a while, and then her mother called us in for dinner.

We sat on the mat, and the food was already on my plate. I was used to eating with my hands, but they used forks and chopsticks. Her two brothers were there too. I wondered where her father was. Later she told me that he worked late and was hardly ever home. The meal was quiet, but I was used to this. I never talked during any of my meals. It was dark by the time we finished.

They all decided that I would sleep on that soft bed. It was king size, but to me it seemed even larger. I was excited because I had never slept on a bed before. Seinique pulled the see-through cloth up and told me to crawl inside. It was so soft. I just lay there and closed my eyes. I liked this place. Seinique then left, and I was soon fast asleep.

In the middle of the night I felt something move the bed. I was a little scared at first. I looked around, and someone was crawling into bed with me. It was Seinique. She lay down beside me and asked me how I was doing. Then she left the room again, and I rolled over and went back to sleep. When I woke up the next morning, I found her beside me again. She was already awake. We went to the room where they ate, and we got breakfast. Ma' Lee had already left, and her brothers were getting on their motorcycles to leave.

Seinique and I spent every waking moment together. We talked about growing up together. I was so happy to be there that I had already forgotten about my old home. I didn't even think about my parents. I spent two weeks with Seinique's family, but it only seemed like a day.

I was sitting outside talking with Seinique when the man on the motorcycle came to her house again. He asked for Ma' Lee, and Seinique went to get her. Ma' Lee came outside, and they talked for a few minutes. He told me that I was going to be taken to another place. Seinique did not like this at all, and she threw a tantrum. I had never seen anyone so upset. It took Ma' Lee a long time to calm her down. Seinique then rushed over and wrapped me in her arms. I had never been hugged like that before, so I just stood there. Deep down inside I really liked the hug, and for the first time I felt that someone really cared about me and loved me. I was leaving again, and I didn't know why. I wished that someone would explain to me what was happening.

The man put me on the motorcycle, and we left. We rode for about twenty minutes through the city. I saw big tall buildings, many cars, and many people. I was fascinated with my surroundings. I had never seen so many people out walking. I wondered what they were all doing. There were signs here and there, but I couldn't read them. In school I had learned to write my name and learned a few interesting facts, but I had left before I could learn anything else.

Orphanage

កន្លែងរក្សាក្មេងកំព្រា

At the end of the ride, we passed a long white wall on our left. We came to a gate in the wall, and we rode inside. There was a big white building on the left, and a fair-skinned lady with blond hair was standing at the side of the building. She came over and talked to the man on the motorcycle for a minute. Then he left, and she walked me to another building. She told me to wait there, and went back into the first building. I looked around, and I saw a bush beside me. I started picking leaves off it, and I sighed. I couldn't believe this was happening again. Why was I being dropped off at another place? I felt warm drops roll down my cheeks, and I realized that I was crying.

I was upset, frustrated, and confused. I wanted to know why I was here, and why I couldn't live forever with my friend Seinique. I thought about my old home. What were my mother and father doing? Did they miss me? Did they care about me or know where I was? I wondered if they were the reason I was here. Then another lady came out of the building where I was sitting and asked me why I was crying. I didn't answer her. She told me to come inside.

Inside the building there were rows of long tables. No one else was there. The lady got a bowl, filled it with soup, and gave it to me. When I finished eating, she showed me around the place. She told me that her name was Min 'Iep.

To the right about forty feet there was a long building. Min 'Iep walked me over to it and showed me what was inside. There were blankets everywhere. She told me that this was where I was going to sleep. I later learned that the place that I was in was called an orphanage.

That night I wasn't the only one sleeping there. There were about forty or fifty other girls all snuggled close to one another on the floor. I wondered if they were in the same situation as me, taken away from their homes and brought to this strange place.

While I was there, I liked to walk around and explore. Behind the orphanage's main office and to the right of it a bit there were some mango trees. I loved to pick the ripe mangos. I would eat them skin and all, except that I would throw away the seed.

To the right of the mango trees there was a cement *bontúp tuk* (bathroom). Inside there were three individual rooms. Inside each room there was a big hole in the floor where a person could *chu-nóm*. There were no doors, and anyone walking by could see inside. It always smelled so bad there.

A few feet behind the *bontúp tuk* there was the building where the kids ate. Past that building and to the right there was a big open area with a lot of palm trees. To the left there was a water pump, and there was a small structure next to it. It wasn't really a building. It had a roof and two side walls. The ends were open, and people could walk through it. There were towels hanging on hooks on the sides for people to use after taking a bath. Beyond that building, to the left a few yards, was the building where the girls slept. The building where the boys slept was farther back, hidden in the trees.

To the right there was a path that disappeared into the jungle. I liked to explore, and I was always curious about it. I never went far down the path though. I was uneasy about being in an unfamiliar place, and I didn't want to get lost.

One afternoon I was surrounded by a huge crowd of people, and they were all looking upward at something. I looked up, and I saw a man climbing a palm tree. The people started cheering, and they rushed to a certain spot. I moved out of the way, and I saw why the people were rushing around. They all wanted coconuts. When I looked again, I noticed that there were about three men, each climbing a different tree. They would cut the coconuts off the tree and toss them down into the crowd of people. The people would try to catch them as they fell. I don't remember how, but I got one, and someone opened it for me. I liked the crunch as I bit into it. While I was eating it, the fair-skinned lady came up to me and gave me a piece of honeycomb. It was bigger than my hand. I ate it wax and all.

It was very sticky, but I enjoyed it. It was an exciting day for me.

Every day Min 'Iep would make me sit down, and she would take strange small bugs out of my hair. My hair was down to the middle of my back, and it had never been cut. Min 'Iep got frustrated one day and decided that it was time to cut my hair. She told me that it would make taking the bugs out easier. She took hold of my hair, and in a few snips it was gone. She cut it right below my ears and gave me bangs. I didn't like my hair that short. I was upset because I didn't have any say in the matter.

I didn't have any friends at the orphanage. It seemed like they were all off doing their own thing. In the morning I would see some kids who were a few years older than me leaving the orphanage, and I would follow them. I asked them where they were going, and they said that they were going to school. I liked school, and I wanted to go too. The older kids said that I was too young. I tried to explain that I had been to school before, but they wouldn't listen.

Sometimes I would try to sneak out with the other kids, but the grownups that worked at the orphanage caught on to me. They always stopped me from going. I wanted to go to school because there wasn't much to do at the orphanage, and I often got bored.

I found out that Seinique's mom, Ma' Lee, worked at the orphanage. I would go into the main office building and talk with her almost every day. She was always nice, and she would tell me how Seinique was doing. Sometimes I would even see Seinique's brothers there. They always rode into the orphanage on their motorcycles. They remembered me, and whenever they came, they would talk with me for a little while. The younger one especially liked me. He would ask me how I was doing and tell me about Seinique. He said that she missed me very much and wanted to see me again.

She couldn't though, because her mother wouldn't allow her to come to the orphanage.

There was a place at the edge of the jungle where I liked to go. It was in front of the building where the girls slept. There was a tamarind tree there, and I liked to eat the tamarind beans. There weren't that many that I could reach, so I would pick up the ones that had fallen on the ground.

One time when I was picking up a tamarind bean, a boy about eight years old came from behind me. He asked me what I was doing, and I told him. I gave him a tamarind bean. He looked at it, but didn't say anything. Then he started walking down the path that disappeared into the jungle. He turned around and asked me if I wanted to come with him. I thought about it and walked toward him. The boy reached over for my hand, but I got scared and ran away. When I looked back, he was gone. I never saw him again.

One morning when I was walking over to see Ma' Lee, I spotted a girl crying. She was about the same age as me. She had wavy dark brown hair, and she was a bit lighter complected than me. She was sitting near the building where the kids ate. I walked over to her and talked to her for a bit. I tried to cheer her up, and I asked her if she wanted to play a game. She did, and we ran around playing for a little while. Then she had to go *chu-nóm*, so I showed her where the *bontúp tuk* was.

While I waited, I sat down next to the building where the kids ate and started picking small leaves off the bushes. Then I heard a motorcycle come up behind me. I looked to see who it was, hoping that it might be one of Seinique's brothers. Instead, to my disappointment, it was the man on the motorcycle. When I looked closer, I realized that it was a different man, one that I didn't know. He told me to get on the motorcycle with him, and I did. I wondered where I was being taken now. It seemed like I was going to be moving from place to place for the rest of my life. I didn't understand why.

I tried to look around at my surroundings, but the motorcycle moved too fast. I was on the motorcycle for several hours when we came to a dirt road. We turned down that road and rode on for a few more hours, but it seemed like days. Soon I was drifting from awake to asleep, but every time I fell asleep, a bump in the road would jolt me awake.

We finally reached a house, and a lady came out and ran toward me. She started crying. She wrapped her arms around me and told me how sorry she was for giving me away. She said that she missed me very much and loved me. I was really confused. I had never seen this lady in my entire life. She turned my face toward hers so she could look at me. Then she realized that she wasn't talking to her daughter. The smile faded from her face, and she started yelling at the man. She told him to take me back and bring back her real daughter. I felt rejected at that moment, and I didn't know why. I didn't even know this lady, but what she said made me feel sad. Then the man realized his mistake. He was very embarrassed, and he apologized to the woman many times.

We got back on the motorcycle, and it was another long ride back to the orphanage. The man apologized to me, and he told me his name was Paa Ti'. He said that he thought I was the lady's daughter because I hadn't complained about getting on the motorcycle or asked why I was leaving. When we got back to the orphanage, he gave me some money. It was after dark, and everyone else was asleep.

The fair-skinned lady came running out of the main office. She looked worried about something. She ran over to me and wrapped me in her arms, but this hug was very quick. She seemed relieved to see me. She thought that I had been kidnapped or had run away. Then I noticed a girl with the fair-skinned lady. It was the same one that I had been playing with earlier. Paa Ti' had accidentally gotten me mixed up with her. In the end everything was straightened out, and the girl got to go home to her mother. Then I was sent to bed. It was late, and I was exhausted. I was glad to sleep.

One afternoon I was sitting outside with a group of kids watching a television. It was very hot, and we were sitting under a thatched roof. This was the first time I had ever seen a television. On the television screen some men were chasing a young woman through the jungle. They caught up to her, and they tied her to a tree. They asked her some questions, but I guess they didn't like her responses because the next thing that happened was that they cut her tongue out. I was horrified by this. I could not imagine anyone doing something like that. The woman was about twenty-two years old, and she was gorgeous. She had perfectly straight black hair, very light skin, and dark brown eyes.

Then the scene changed, and another young woman just as gorgeous came running through the jungle. She saw the woman who had gotten her tongue cut out tied to the tree, and she untied her. Her friend was trying to warn her of something, but she couldn't speak, so that didn't help much. Out of nowhere the men came back and caught the new woman. The first woman escaped in the nick of time. They tied the new woman to a tree and started questioning her. Then they cut her tongue out too. I could not believe that this was happening. I didn't know that it was being acted out.

Then someone came from behind me and picked me up, and I didn't get to see what happened next. It was one of Seinique's brothers. They were both there. They told me that it wasn't good for me to have seen that movie. They started to tickle me, and they laughed and smiled. They talked to me for a while, and then they got on their motorcycles and went home.

The younger one would visit me more often. I didn't see the older one that much, and he never had much to say. He seemed a bit shy, but he was always smiling. They were the nicest boys I had ever met.

A few weeks later I was walking around looking for something to do. I was walking past the building where the kids ate when I heard some noise. I walked into the building, and to my surprise, there were a lot of kids inside. They were all lined up and separated into groups. The boys were on one side, and the girls were on the other side. I looked to the head of the line, and there were some grownups that looked French that I had never seen before.

Then Min 'Iep came over and told me that she had been looking for me everywhere. She took me to the head of the line where the other girls were standing and tossed me a purple dress. She told me to put it on. I did, but it was much too big for me.

A French man stood me by a wall and told me to stand still. Suddenly there was a big flash, and the room seemed to become dark for a few seconds. Then Min 'Iep told me to take the dress off, and I did. I was still squinting a bit as my eyes adjusted to the dark room. Min 'Iep gave the dress to the next girl in line, and the same thing happened to her. I later learned that these kids were getting their pictures taken so they could be adopted. No one had ever told me about that though. After watching the process happen several times, I lost interest and left to see what other things I could find to do.

A New Beginning

ការចាប់ផ្ដើមថ្មី

There was one particular day that I was going to visit Ma' Lee. I was walking toward the main office building when I spotted her by the mango trees. I went over to her, and we talked for a little while. Then we walked to the main office building together. There were several people standing outside. One of them was the fair-skinned lady. She walked up to me and said that one of the men was my father. I looked up to the man she had pointed to. He was the tallest and lightest complected person I had ever seen. I felt shy and didn't know exactly how to react, so I hid behind Ma' Lee's legs. I knew that he was not my father because he looked nothing like me. She kept insisting that he was indeed my father. I didn't know it at the time, but I was being adopted.

Ma' Lee and the fair-skinned lady took me to where the water pump was located. They told me to take a bath. Two older girls were there who had just finished taking a bath. They were about sixteen years old. When I was done, the fair-skinned lady told them to get me a towel. One of them handed me hers. I dried myself off, and the fair-skinned lady gave me some new clothes. She gave me a floral purple dress, a white top, and a pair of underwear. That was the first time I had worn underwear. Then we headed back to the office.

Once we got inside, I sat down in a chair and watched what was going on. My new dad gave me a stuffed monkey. I took it, but I wasn't sure what to say. I was confused about what was happening. My new dad held his camera up to take a picture of me. I sat up straight for him because by then I knew what to do when someone took pictures of me. Then he picked me up into his arms, and the fair-skinned lady took a picture of us with Ma' Lee. I couldn't believe how high off the ground I was. Another lady that worked in the orphanage office took a picture of the three of us with the fair-skinned lady. I couldn't comprehend all the information that I had just received. I just wanted everything to be normal again. I wanted to be with my best friend Seinique.

Next thing I knew, I was leaving in a car with my new dad. That was the first time I had ever ridden in a car, and I was curious about where I was going next. I sat on my new dad's lap throughout the whole ride. The driver's name was Pol, and he took us to a French doctor. The doctor examined me and spoke to my new dad in a language I didn't understand. Then Pol took us to a pharmacy where my new dad got some medicine for me. From there, Pol took us to the Tai Seng Hotel. I had never been to a hotel before. When we got to our room, I fell asleep. There was just too much to think about.

When I woke up, we went to eat lunch at a restaurant called the Seven Seven. It was only a block away from the hotel. After lunch a new driver named Sunny came and took us to a market. My new dad bought me a pair of shoes, a green *krama* (Cambodian shawl), a T-shirt with the Cambodian flag on it, and a few Cambodian tapes. I had always wanted to go to a market, and I enjoyed it. There were so many people and things to see. It was an amazing atmosphere.

After we left the market, Sunny dropped us off at the American Embassy. My new dad had to get some paperwork done there. I didn't understand why though. While we waited, he asked me if I had to go to the *bontúp tuk*. There was a young lady nearby who heard him speak to me in Cambodian. She laughed like it was the funniest thing she had ever heard. I thought this was strange. I didn't see anything funny about it.

I went in, and instead of sitting down on the toilet, at first I just stood there facing it. I had never been taught how to use a toilet, and I had a difficult time. Somehow I managed to sit on the toilet, but facing the wrong way. In the end everything worked out.

Later, Sunny picked us up and took us back to the hotel. We stayed there for a little while, and then we walked to the Seven Seven to eat dinner. It was almost dark then. On the way, an old man on the street came up to me. He asked me to come with him, and I got scared. He tried to grab me, but

I was too fast for him. I got away and hurried to catch up with my new dad. On the way back to the hotel he was still on the street, but this time he just watched me.

Back at the hotel I soon got bored, so I went out in the hall and started walking up and down the stairs. One time I walked into another family's room. They were also Americans who were adopting. They were nice and didn't mind me being there. Then my new dad and I went down to the lobby where I noticed a big fish tank. I had always been fascinated by fish. I slapped the glass to make the fish swim about.

When we got back to our room, my new dad rubbed some medicine on my arms for scabies. I didn't like the medicine. It hurt, and I whimpered. Later that evening the fair-skinned lady came to the hotel and gave him some shampoo to take the bugs out of my hair. When she left, he washed my hair with the shampoo. Then he combed the bugs out of my hair. It was late, and I was getting sleepy. Several times I would almost fall over, and then I would wake up again.

The next morning we ate breakfast at the Seven Seven. Then we went back to the hotel, and my new dad called Sunny. While we waited, he took some pictures of the hotel and the surrounding area.

A little later Sunny came and picked us up. He drove us around trying to find a place where my new dad could get our plane tickets taken care of to go to America. We stopped at a big white building that had a lion statue by the door. We went inside, and somebody there gave us directions to the right place. It was kind of like an adventure, driving from place to place in the city. It was all new and interesting.

Along the way, Sunny had to get gas for his car, so we stopped at a Total gas station. I didn't know why the car needed to be filled up. We came back to the hotel, and I slept for a while. I was not used to running around so much.

When I woke up, my new dad gave me some crayons and a notebook. I just stared at it. I had no idea what to do with it. He took a crayon out and made a mark on the paper. Then he looked at me and gave me the crayon. I took it, marked the paper the same way he had, and put the crayon down. I didn't see anything interesting about it.

That evening Sunny took us to an open-air nightclub restaurant. It was built on stilts above the Mekong River. It was absolutely beautiful. There were lights across the river reflecting on the water, making it look even more beautiful. I watched the lights for a long time. I was intrigued by them.

There were two young ladies at the front of the restaurant. They danced slowly as they sang. A man came by selling flashlights that were shaped like a lotus flower. They had plastic fibers about six inches long extending out from the middle of them. The fibers were lit up with different colors. A few of the plastic fibers had small white flowers attached to them. My new dad bought me one, and I liked it instantly. He and Sunny talked while we were eating, but I didn't understand what they were saying. This didn't bother me because I was too busy thinking about all the events that had unfolded before me these past few days.

The next morning we ate breakfast at the Seven Seven again. When we finished, we went to the Seven Seven Store, right above the restaurant. My new dad bought a few food items, and we went back to the hotel and started packing. Then Sunny came and took us to the airport. At the airport, he came in with us. We talked a while, and someone took a picture of the three of us. Before he left, Sunny gave me a Cambodian tape. The cover had a picture of a soldier, and in the background more were falling from the sky with parachutes.

We looked around the airport shops for a while, and my new dad bought a couple souvenirs. When it was time to board the airplane, we had to walk outside and up some steps to get into the plane. There was a pretty flight attendant, and she gave me a pink and white stuffed bear. It was the softest thing I had ever touched. I liked it as soon as I got it.

While I was sitting in my seat, my new dad tried to put the seat belt on me. I didn't know what was going on, and I wouldn't let him fasten it. I didn't like having something strapping me down. I didn't know why I needed it in the first place. Finally he managed to fasten it, but I tried to pull it off again. We repeated this several times. Eventually I gave up and settled down. I looked out the window, and I was fascinated by what I saw.

When the plane took off, I felt my body lean back, and my stomach felt like it was floating. It was a strange feeling. I felt a little uneasy, and I didn't know what to expect. I looked out the window again, and there were fields of crops that extended out as far as I could see. It was so pretty. I never knew that things could look so small and far away. The sight was amazing, and I absorbed as much of it as I could.

A couple hours later we arrived at the airport in Singapore. There were so many things happening and so many people rushing around. I felt even smaller here. We looked around the airport and went into some shops. There was a train that connected the two terminals called the Sky Train. We rode it to the other terminal and back. I enjoyed the short train ride, and I wanted to ride it over and over again.

When we ate lunch, my new dad met some people that had adopted a baby girl from Cambodia named Macaraa. They gave me a key chain. It was a purple egg-shaped thing. I pressed the button on the end, and the cover popped open. Inside were three pigs, two baby pigs and a mother. There was a clear plastic dome over the pigs, and the purple cover closed over it. The pigs moved around like they were drinking milk from their mother. I was fascinated by this. I closed it, and it made a clicking sound as it latched. I kept opening it over and over because I liked to watch the pigs move. It boggled my mind to see the pigs move by themselves, and I wondered what made them move.

There was a long time between flights, so my new dad decided to take us on a bus tour of the city of Singapore. A Chinese lady was our guide, and she spoke to the group in a language I didn't understand. The city was beautiful. I had never seen buildings so high. It was cloudy, but they seemed to sparkle with many colors as if the sun had touched down on them. There were cars and motorcycles everywhere. I had never seen so much traffic before.

The bus stopped at the Singapore River, and everybody got off. We got to ride on a boat out on the river, and we got to see the Mer-Lion. It was shaped like a mermaid, but it had a lion's head. It was the largest statue I had ever seen. While we were on the boat, it kept rocking back and forth, and I wasn't exactly sure what to think. My new dad kept trying to get me to smile, but it didn't work. I wasn't sure of what the boat was going to do. Soon the boat turned around, and we returned to the shore. Then we got back on the bus.

Back at the airport, we ate dinner. We had an Indian dish. After dinner we walked around the airport. There was a long narrow pond where there were big orange fish swimming around. There was a bridge that I could walk over and look down at the fish. It was a very pretty airport.

There were moving walkways that I liked to run on. I would run really fast, fall down on my knees, and let the moving walkways move me. It was fun because I never knew that the ground could move like that. I wanted to do this for a long time, but then I remembered the Sky Train, and I wanted to go back and ride it again. I told my new dad, and we did that a few more times.

Then we went to our departure lounge, and we saw the people who had adopted Macaraa again. When we got on the plane, it was after dark. We were surprised to find out that their seats were right in front of ours, and we had a chance to talk to them. I tried to sleep on the plane, and eventually I did, even though it wasn't that comfortable. I had so much to think about. I wondered where I was going next.

Near the end of our flight they served a meal on the plane. They had some meat, mushrooms, and a few other things. I had finished eating all my mushrooms, and I enjoyed them. Then I noticed that my new dad still had some mushrooms. I reached my fork over and started eating them off his plate.

The next morning we landed in Amsterdam. Before we got into the airport, my new dad thought it would be chilly, and he tried to put a jacket on me. I didn't want it because I had never worn more than one item of clothing on top, and it seemed strange to have something else on. Finally he gave up and let me go without it.

Inside the airport we found a McDonald's Playland, and my new dad asked me if I wanted to play with the other kids. I looked out at the kids, and I didn't want to play with them. I was scared that if I went to play with them, my new dad would disappear, and I wondered where I would end up next. He was the only person that I knew and could trust even though I didn't know much about him. I didn't want to keep moving from place to place. I didn't understand anything that was happening, and I didn't understand what people around me were saying. I was tired and confused.

We then got back on the plane that was going to take us to America. During the flight I looked out the window and saw the ocean. I thought it was the biggest river I had ever seen. It was the deepest darkest blue, and it stretched out as far as I could see. I was amazed by this.

When supper was served, I just picked at it. I didn't feel too hungry. A few hours later we landed in the bustling city of New York. My dad told me that we had arrived in America, and we got off the plane.

From there we went through customs. There was an extremely impatient black policeman who was yelling at everyone. I didn't understand what he was saying, but I didn't care. There was something about the way he acted that made me dislike him. We then went to a room where my dad got some papers.

We stayed at the airport for a few more hours waiting for our next flight. Then we got on a plane going to a place called Dallas. There were only six people on the plane including my dad and me. While we were waiting for the plane to leave, a strange sensation came over me. I had never felt anything like it before. It felt like something was coming up my throat. The next thing I knew, there was food everywhere. My dad looked for an airsickness bag, but he couldn't find one. It must have been the only seat on the plane that didn't have one. Then it happened again, and it was all over my clothes. That was the first time I had ever *k'-úot* (thrown up), but I felt a lot better afterward. A flight attendant came over and helped us clean up. She gave me an adult extra large T-shirt to change into, and then we moved to a different seat to get away from the mess.

The rest of the flight to Dallas was uneventful. When we arrived, my dad tried to put a sweatshirt on me. I felt the chill and realized that I needed it, so I let him. We walked around exploring the airport for a while. Then we got on another airplane. This time we were going to a place called El Paso. I wondered how long I would be traveling. It seemed like an eternity.

When we arrived in El Paso, we picked up our bags and went out to my dad's car. He had just buckled me in when that strange sensation came over me again. I whimpered, and he knew what was about to happen. He quickly unbuckled me, and I hurried out of the car and *k'-úot* again. When we left, my dad drove slowly in case we might have to stop along the way.

When we arrived at my new home, my dad asked me what I thought of it. Then that strange sensation came over me again. He heard me whimper, and he rushed me into the *bontúp tuk*. We tried to get ready for bed, but I *k'-úot* several more times. It wasn't until 3:00 in the morning that we finally got to sleep.

I was exhausted from the trip, and it felt good to lie down. I had been traveling for thirty hours nonstop. I closed my eyes, thinking that everything that had happened was just a dream. I thought that I would wake up back in Cambodia, and everything would be the same again. Everything that had happened was too much to think about, and I couldn't comprehend it all.

When I woke up the next day, I was more rested and felt a lot better. I looked around, and I was still in the same place. Maybe this wasn't a dream after all.

Epilogue

ការនិយាយបញ្ចប់

My entire world had been turned upside down, and what I thought about life would be changed forever. Everything was so different at my new home. The people spoke, looked, and acted differently. I was amazed at everything I saw. I got to go to school again, and I soon had many friends.

For the first time I felt a sense of belonging, and I was happy to be where I was. My father and his family loved me like I had never been loved before. I finally had a place that I could call home. A place where I felt loved and wanted.

Some day I hope to go back to Cambodia. I hope to find my old home and look for my hidden treasures. I would like to find my friends again and see how much things have changed. I will always remember my old home and the people who changed my life there. I'm happy in my new life, but I will never forget all the exciting adventures I had in Cambodia.

Acknowledgements

ការដឹងគុណ

Thanks to:

GOD for keeping me safe and showing
His irrevocable love for me.

My father for helping me to write this book.

My amazing family for accepting me more
than I ever could have asked for.

All my awesome friends who have made my life
even more amazing.

Narith Lim for helping with the
Cambodian translations.